Dog Treat Recipes

By
Sharon Gick

Published by Pet Qwerks, Inc.

101 DOG TREATS
BY
SHARON GICK

Dogs are healthiest and happiest when they have a proper and consistent diet. Occasional treats made from natural, healthy ingredients can be a wonderful way of rewarding our pets.

Healthy Ingredients:

The recipes in this book have been created with health in mind. Though the recipe may be named Cheesy Balls they actually contain little cheese. Moderation is the key to keeping the treats and your dog healthy. It doesn't need to be high fat in order to please your dog. After all, from Spot's perspective, much of the goodness in a treat is the display of your approval by rewarding him. So, when it comes to ingredients like cheese, bacon, etc. use them in small quantities. Keep in mind that dogs can smell 100 times better than humans.

On storing treats:

Many of the treats shown in this book are perishable. The fruit and meat recipes can be especially short lived. Treats should be refrigerated if not consumed within a week. If you wish to store them longer than a week they should be frozen. In general, dry treats will not perish as quickly as moist treats.

Published by:
Pet Qwerks, Inc.
9 Studebaker Dr., Irvine, CA 92618

www.petqwerks.com

www.facebook.com/petqwerks

ISBN 978-0-615-55360-3
Printed in China

TABLE OF CONTENTS

CHEWY BACON COOKIES

Ingredients:
1 cup whole-wheat flour
1 cup rolled oats
1 tsp. baking powder
1 tbsp. honey
1 tsp. vanilla extract
1 cup chicken broth, low-sodium
1 egg
6 slices bacon, cooked & crumbled

Directions:
Preheat oven to 350°F. Lightly spray cookie sheet with nonstick cooking spray.

In a bowl, stir flour, rolled oats, baking powder and bacon. Stir in chicken broth, honey, vanilla and egg until soft dough forms. Drop spoonfuls onto greased cookie sheet and gently flatten using a fork. You can make large cookies for big dogs or little cookies for the tiny breeds.

Bake for about 15 minutes or until golden brown.

CHEESY CHICKEN SQUARES

Ingredients:
2 cups whole wheat flour
1 tsp. garlic powder
½ cup Parmesan cheese, grated
1 cup chicken, cooked & shredded
1 tbsp. oil
1 egg
1 tsp. chicken bouillon
½ cup water

Directions:
Preheat oven to 350°F. Lightly spray cookie sheet with nonstick cooking spray.

Combine all ingredients in a large bowl. Mix well until dough is formed. On a floured surface, knead the dough for 2-3 minutes. Roll out to 1/2 inch thick and cut into squares. A pizza cutter works great for cutting rolled dough. Place squares onto greased cookie sheet. Bake for about 15 minutes or until light brown.

CHEESE SHELLS

Ingredients:
Dough:
1 cup whole wheat flour
1 cup cornmeal
1 tsp. baking powder
1 tsp. chicken bouillon

½ cup water
1 egg, beaten

Filling:
1 cup Cheddar cheese, shredded

Directions:
Preheat oven 375°F. Spray muffin pan with nonstick cooking spray.

Combine all dough ingredients in a bowl. Mix well until dough is formed. Onto a floured surface, knead dough for 2-3 minutes. Roll into 1/4 inch thickness and cut into rounds.

Press each dough rounds onto the bottom and up the sides of the greased muffin cups. Add the cheese onto each biscuit and press slightly with your fingers. Bake for 10-15 minutes or until done.

CHICKEN RICE ROLLS

Ingredients:
1 cup whole wheat flour
1 cup rice flour
½ cup brown rice, cooked
½ cup chicken, cooked & shredded
¼ cup carrots, shredded
¼ cup green beans, cooked
1 tbsp. olive oil
1 egg
¾ cup chicken broth, low-sodium

Directions:
Preheat oven to 350°F. Lightly spray cookie sheet with nonstick cooking spray. In a food processor, puree rice, chicken, carrots, beans, oil, egg and chicken broth. Set aside.

In a large bowl, combine the flours and add the pureed mixture. Mix well until dough is formed. On a floured surface, knead the dough for 3-4 minutes. Roll out to 1/8 inch thickness and cut into squares. Brush squares with water to make surface sticky. Roll squares into tubes. Place rolls on a greased baking sheet. Bake for about 20 minutes or until golden brown.

BEET BALLS

Ingredients:
1 cup whole wheat flour
1 cup oatmeal
½ cup cheddar cheese, shredded
½ cup frozen peas, thawed
½ cup carrots, shredded
½ cup brown rice, cooked
1 egg

1 tbsp. oil
½ cup chicken broth, low sodium
½ cup beet juice for garnish

Directions:
Preheat oven to 350°F. Lightly spray cookie sheet with nonstick cooking spray.

In a blender, puree peas, carrots, rice, egg, oil and chicken broth. Set aside.

In a bowl, combine cheese, oatmeal and flour. Stir in the pureed mixture. Mix well until sticky dough is formed. Pinch a table spoon and roll into balls. Place balls onto greased cookie sheet. Bake for 10-15 minutes.

Remove from oven. Dip balls into beet juice and return to oven for 2-3 minutes to dry. This will give you some delicious faux Italian meatballs.

CHEESY SAUSAGE BALLS

Ingredients:
1 cup whole wheat flour
1 tsp. baking powder
1 tsp. chicken bouillon
½ lb. turkey sausage, cooked & chopped
¼ cup Cheddar cheese, shredded
1 egg
¼ cup water
2 tbsp. oil

Directions:
Preheat oven to 350°F. Lightly spray cookie sheet with nonstick cooking spray.

Combine all ingredients in a large bowl. Mix thoroughly. Pinch a table-spoon and roll into balls about 1 inch diameter. Place balls onto greased cookie sheet.

Bake for 15-20 minutes or until golden brown.

CHICKEN CAKES

Ingredients:
1 cup whole wheat flour
1 cup oatmeal
2 tbsp. oil
1 egg
¼ cup milk, nonfat
¼ cup water
1 cup chicken, cooked & shredded
1 tsp. chicken bouillon
1 tbsp. parsley, fresh & minced

Directions:
Preheat oven to 350°F. Lightly spray cookie sheet with nonstick cooking spray.

In a bowl, combine all ingredients. Mix well until stiff dough is formed. Onto floured surface, knead dough for 2-3 minutes. Roll out into 1/2 inch thick and cut with round cookie cutter. Place cookies onto greased cookie sheet.

Bake for 15-20 minutes or until golden brown.

DOGGY MEATLOAF

Ingredients:

1 cup whole-wheat flour
1 cup oatmeal
½ lb. ground turkey
½ cup carrots, shredded
½ cup green beans
1 egg

2 tbsp. olive oil
1 tsp. chicken bouillon
½ cup milk, fat-free
1 tsp. fresh parsley, minced
½ cup Parmesan cheese, shredded

Directions:

Preheat oven to 350°F. Lightly spray baking sheet with nonstick cooking spray.

In a food processor, puree carrots, beans, egg, oil, milk, chicken bouillon and parsley. Transfer the mixture to a large bowl. Slowly add flour, oatmeal, cheese and ground turkey. Mix thoroughly. Place onto greased cookie sheet and mold into the shape of a meatloaf.

Bake for 30 minutes or until done. Allow to cool and slice with serrated knife to the desired thickness.

HAMMY PUPPERS

Ingredients:
1 ½ cups whole wheat flour
½ cup rolled oats
2 tsp. cinnamon
1 tbsp. honey
1 egg
½ cup applesauce, unsweetened
½ cup ham, cooked & diced
½ cup milk, low-fat

Directions:
Preheat oven to 350°F. Line mini muffin pan with mini muffin paper cups. Lightly spray muffin cups with nonstick cooking spray.

In a large bowl, stir honey, egg, applesauce, 1/4 cup of ham and milk. Add cinnamon, flour and oats. Mix well. Pour batter evenly into greased muffin cups. Lightly press the remaining ¼ cup of ham pieces into the top of puppers. Bake for 15-20 minutes.

HONEY BACON MUFFINS

Ingredients:

2 cups whole wheat flour
1 tsp. baking powder
2 tbsp. honey
1 egg, lightly beaten

1 tbsp. canola oil
1 cup chicken broth, low-sodium
4 pcs. bacon, cooked & crumbled*

Directions:
Preheat oven to 350°F. Lightly spray muffin pan with nonstick cooking spray.

Combine all ingredients in a large bowl. Mix well until thoroughly blended. Pour batter evenly into greased muffin pan.

Bake for 20-25 minutes or until golden on top.

*As always when using meats, be sure to cook thoroughly and drain all excess fats.

LITTLE PIZZA PIES

Ingredients:

Dough:
2 cups whole wheat flour
1 tsp. baking powder
1 egg
½ cup chicken broth, low-sodium

Toppings:
½ cup Mozzarella cheese, shredded
¼ cup chicken, cooked & shredded
¼ cup bacon, cooked & crumbled
¼ cup tomato paste

Directions:

Preheat oven to 350°F. Lightly spray cookie sheet with nonstick cooking spray.

Combine dough ingredients in a bowl. Mix well until a stiff dough is formed. Onto a floured surface, knead dough for 3 minutes. Roll into ¼ inch thickness and cut into rounds appropriately sized for your dog. Transfer rounds onto a greased cookie sheet. Use a spoon to spread tomato paste on rounds. Add remaining topping ingredients.

Bake for 20 minutes or until done.

FLAXSEED STICKS

Ingredients:
Dough:
1 cup whole wheat flour
1 cup oat flour
1 tsp. chicken bouillon
1 tbsp. oil
½ cup water
1 tbsp. molasses
1 egg, beaten

Filling:
¼ cup flaxseed*
¼ cup wheat germ
⅛ cup Parmesan cheese, grated
1 egg white, for egg wash

Directions:
Preheat oven to 350°F. Lightly spray baking sheet with nonstick cooking spray.

Combine all dough ingredients. Mix well until dough is formed. Onto floured surface, knead dough for 3 minutes. Roll out into rectangle about 1/8 inch thick. Brush with egg wash and cut dough into half. Set aside.

In a separate bowl, mix cheese, wheat germ, and flaxseed. Spread flaxseed filling evenly over half of the dough and lay second dough on top egg wash side down. Press together with rolling pin. Brush top with egg wash again and sprinkle with flaxseed. Cut dough into strips using sharp knife or pizza cutter. Place into greased baking sheet. Bake for about 10 minutes or until browned on top.

*Flaxseed is an excellent source of alpha-linolenic acid, a type of Omega-3 fatty acid that is critical for your pet's skin and coat health. It can prevent dry, itchy skin and shedding.

MAC & CHEESE ROLLUPS

Ingredients:
2 cups whole wheat flour
1 cup whole grain macaroni pasta, cooked
1 cup cheddar cheese, shredded
1 tbsp. margarine
6 oz. plain yogurt
½ cup chicken broth, low-sodium

Directions:
Preheat oven to 350°F. Lightly spray baking sheet with nonstick cooking spray.

In a food processor, blend in pasta, cheese, margarine, yogurt and chicken broth. Transfer to a large bowl. Stir in flour. Mix well until soft dough is formed. On a floured surface, knead dough for 3 minutes. Roll dough out to 1/8 inch thickness and cut into appropriately sized squares. Brush squares with water to make surface sticky. Roll squares into tubes. Place rolls on a greased baking sheet.

Bake for 15-20 minutes or until golden brown.

THREE CHEESE MINI BITES

Ingredients:
2 cups whole wheat flour
¼ cup Cheddar cheese, shredded
¼ cup Parmesan cheese, grated
¼ cup Jack cheese, shredded
1 tsp. fresh parsley, minced
½ cup chicken broth, low-sodium
1 tbsp. oil

Directions:
Preheat oven to 350°F. Lightly spray baking sheet with nonstick cooking spray.

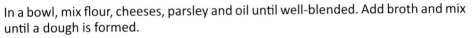

In a bowl, mix flour, cheeses, parsley and oil until well-blended. Add broth and mix until a dough is formed.

Onto a floured surface, knead the dough and roll out to 1/4 inch thick. Cut out dough into tiny squares with a knife or pizza cutter. Place on a greased cookie sheet. Bake for 10-12 minutes or until lightly browned.

ROLLED HAM & CHEESE

Ingredients:
Dough:
1 cup whole wheat flour
1 cup oatmeal
1 egg
¼ cup applesauce, unsweetened
¼ cup milk, fat-free

Filling:
¼ cup cheddar cheese, cut in strips
¼ cup ham, cooked & cut in strips

Directions:
Preheat oven to 350°F. Spray baking sheet with nonstick cooking spray.

Combine all dough ingredients and mix well until dough forms. On a floured surface, knead the dough for about 3 minutes. Roll out into ¼ inch thickness and cut into appropriately sized squares. Brush dough with water and top with ham and cheese. Roll into tubes and press ends with your hands to seal. Place into greased baking sheet. Bake for 20-25 minutes or until brown.

BACON & SWISS STICKS

Ingredients:
1 cup whole wheat flour
1 cup oat flour
½ cup Swiss cheese, shredded
1 egg
½ cup chicken broth
4 slices bacon, cooked & crumbled

Directions:
Preheat oven to 350°F. Spray baking sheet with nonstick cooking spray.

In a large bowl, stir in chicken broth, egg, bacon and cheese. Add flours and mix well until stiff dough is formed. On a floured surface, knead the dough for 3 minutes and roll out into ¼ inch thickness. Cut into strips using pizza cutter or knife. Place strips into greased baking sheet.

Bake for 15 minutes or until edges are golden brown.

BEET & CHEESE TREATS

Ingredients:
1 cup whole wheat flour
1 cup oatmeal
1 tsp. baking powder
¼ cup Cheddar cheese, shredded
¼ cup applesauce, unsweetened
¼ cup milk, fat-free
1 egg, beaten
½ cup beet juice for garnish

Directions:
Preheat oven to 350°F. Spray baking sheet with nonstick cooking spray.

Combine flour, oatmeal, baking powder and cheese in a large bowl. Add egg, applesauce and milk. Mix well until dough is formed.   Onto a floured surface, knead the dough for 3 minutes and roll out to 1/2 inch thick. Cut into triangles. Place into greased baking sheet.

Bake for 15 minutes. Remove from oven and allow to cool. Dip into beet juice, return to oven and bake for 2-3 minutes to dry.

CHEESE EMPANADAS

Ingredients:
2 cups whole wheat flour
1 tsp. chicken bouillon
¼ cup Mozzarella cheese, shredded
1 tbsp. oil
1 egg
½ cup water

Directions:
Preheat oven to 350°F. Spray baking sheet with nonstick cooking spray.

In a bowl, stir flour, chicken bouillon, oil, egg and water until dough forms. On floured surface, knead dough for 3 minutes. Roll dough to 1/8 inch thickness. Cut into rounds and brush with water. Spoon cheese in the middle of the rounds and fold. Press edges together using fork. Place onto greased baking sheet. Bake for 20 minutes or until brown.

HARVEST POPOVERS

Ingredients:
2 cups whole wheat flour
1 tsp. baking powder
1 tsp. chicken bouillon
1 cup Cheddar cheese, shredded
1 ½ cup carrot juice
1 egg

Directions:
Preheat oven to 350°F. Spray mini muffin pan with nonstick cooking spray. Place muffin pan in the oven for several minutes to preheat.

In a large bowl, whisk egg and carrot juice thoroughly. Stir in flour, baking powder, cheese and chicken bouillon. Mix well.

Remove muffin pan from the oven. Quickly fill the hot muffin pan with batter and immediately return to oven.

Bake for 20 minutes or until top is golden brown.

HAM & PEAS COOKIES

Ingredients:
1 cup whole wheat flour
2 cups oatmeal
¼ cup green peas, cooked
½ cup cottage cheese
1 cup water
1 tbsp. oil
1 egg
¼ cup ham, cooked & diced

Directions:
Preheat oven to 350°F. Spray cookie sheet with nonstick cooking spray.

In a large bowl, mix flour, oatmeal, peas, cottage cheese, water, oil and egg until soft dough is formed. Stir in ham and mix well. Onto greased cookie sheet, drop dough by tablespoonfuls and press lightly with fork to flatten.

Bake for 20-25 minutes or until done.

PAWSTA PUCKS

Ingredients:
2 cups whole wheat flour
1 cup whole wheat pasta, cooked
½ cup tomato paste
2 tbsp. olive oil
1 ¼ cup chicken broth, low-sodium

Directions:
In a food processor, blend in pasta, tomato paste and oil. Transfer pureed mixture to a large bowl and stir in flour and chicken broth. Mix well until stiff dough forms. Onto floured surface, divide dough into fourths and shape dough into rolls about 1 inch diameter. Wrap rolls in plastic wrap and chill in the freezer for an hour or until firm.

Heat oven to 350°F. Lightly spray baking sheet with nonstick cooking spray. Remove rolls from plastic wrap. Cut the roll into 1/2 inch slices. Place on greased baking sheet. Bake for 20-25 minutes or until golden brown.

The roll of dough can be stored in the freezer for up to 1 month. For easy treats, just thaw, slice and bake. You're 20 minutes away from having fresh homemade Pawsta Pucks for your pet.

PARMESAN SQUARES

Ingredients:
2 cups whole wheat flour
1 cup oatmeal
1 cup wheat germ
1 tbsp. chicken bouillon
2 tbsp. oil
1 cup water
1 tbsp. honey
1 egg, beaten
¼ cup Parmesan cheese, grated

Directions:
Preheat oven to 350°F. Lightly spray baking sheet with nonstick cooking spray.

Combine flour, oatmeal, wheat germ and chicken bouillon in a large bowl. Stir in oil, water and honey. Mix well until dough forms. Onto a floured surface, knead the dough for 3 minutes. Roll out into 1/2 inch thick and cut into squares. Place squares onto greased baking sheet.

Bake for about 15 minutes or until lightly browned. Allow to cool for several minutes. Dip squares into egg and sprinkle Parmesan cheese on top. Bake for another 5 minutes to dry.

TORT STRIPS

Ingredients:
Flour Tortillas
½ cup Cheddar cheese, shredded

Directions:
This is one of the easiest and simplest treats to make. Simply sprinkle cheese onto a tortilla and cover with another tortilla. Melt cheese in a microwave or in a pan. Flip and heat reverse side. Press together with spatula. Slice into strips using pizza cutter or sharp knife. Use as a hot or cold treat for your pet.

THREE POINTED STAR

Ingredients:
2 cups whole wheat flour
1 cup oatmeal
1 cup wheat germ
2 tsp. baking powder
½ cup Cheddar cheese, shredded
2 tbsp. oil
1 egg, beaten
1 cup water
½ cup ham, cooked & diced

Directions:
Preheat oven to 350°F. Lightly spray baking sheet with nonstick cooking spray.

Combine flour, oatmeal, wheat germ, cheese and baking powder in a large bowl. Stir in oil, egg, water and ham until dough forms. Onto a floured surface, knead dough for 3 minutes. Roll out into ½ inch thick and cut into triangles using a pizza cutter or sharp knife. Bake for 20 minutes or until lightly browned.

HAM TATERS

Ingredients:
1 cup whole wheat flour
1 egg
1 tbsp. oil
¼ cup milk, fat-free
½ cup Cheddar cheese, shredded
½ cup ham, cooked & diced
½ cup sweet potato, cooked & mashed
1 tsp. fresh parsley, minced

Directions:
Preheat oven to 350°F. Lightly grease muffin pan with nonstick cooking spray.

In a bowl, stir in flour, egg, oil and milk until dough forms. Onto floured surface, knead dough for 3 minutes. Roll out into 1/8 inch thick and cut into rounds. Press each rounds into the bottom and up the sides of greased muffin pan.

In a separate bowl, combine sweet potato, ham, cheese and parsley. Mix well. Spoon sweet potato mixture into prepared muffin cup.

Bake for 20-25 minutes or until browned.

TUNA YAM TREATS

Ingredients:
2 cups whole wheat flour
2 cups oatmeal
1 cup sweet potato, cooked & mashed
1 (8oz.) can of tuna packed in water
1 cup applesauce, unsweetened
1 tsp. vanilla

Directions:
Preheat oven to 350°F. Lightly spray baking sheet with non stick cooking spray.

Combine all ingredients in a large bowl. Mix well until dough forms. Onto a floured surface, knead dough for 3 minutes. Roll out into 1/8 inch thick and cut with cookie cutters. Place on a greased baking sheet. Bake for 15 minutes or until golden brown.

TUNA RICE TREATS

Ingredients:
1 cup whole wheat flour
1 cup rice flour
½ cup brown rice, cooked
½ cup tuna, canned in water
¼ cup carrots, shredded
1 tbsp. olive oil
1 egg
¾ cup chicken broth, low-sodium

Directions:
In a food processor, blend in rice, tuna, carrots, oil, egg and chicken broth. Transfer pureed mixture to a large bowl and stir in flours. Mix well until stiff dough forms. Onto floured surface, divide dough into fourths and shape dough into rolls, about 1 inch diameter. Wrap

rolls in plastic wrap and chill in the freezer for an hour or until firm. Heat oven to 350°F. Lightly spray baking sheet with nonstick cooking spray. Remove rolls from plastic wrap. Cut roll into 1/2 inch slices. Place on greased baking sheet.

Bake for 20-25 minutes or until firm.

PARMESAN-HERB ROLLS

Ingredients:
1 cup whole wheat flour
1 cup oat flour
1 tsp. chicken bouillon
1 tsp. fresh parsley, minced
1 tsp. fresh basil, minced
1 tsp. fresh oregano, minced
1 tbsp. oil
½ cup water
1 tbsp. honey
¼ cup Parmesan cheese, grated
1 egg, beaten

Directions:
Combine all ingredients in a large bowl. Mix well until dough forms. Onto floured surface, divide dough into fourths and shape dough into rolls about 1 inch diameter. Wrap rolls in plastic wrap and chill in the freezer until firm.

Heat oven to 350°F. Lightly spray baking sheet with non stick cooking spray. Remove rolls from plastic wrap. Cut the rolls into 1/2 inch slices. Place on greased baking sheet. Bake for 20-25 minutes or until golden brown.

CHEDDAR CRUNCHIES

Ingredients:
2 cups whole wheat flour
2 cups Shredded Wheat, spoon sized
¼ cup Cheddar cheese, shredded
¼ cup brown rice, cooked
1 ⅛ cups water
1 tsp. chicken bouillon
1 egg

Directions:
Preheat oven to 350°F. Lightly spray baking sheet with nonstick cooking spray.

Combine water and Shredded Wheat. Set aside for about 10 minutes. Add flour, cheese, rice, chicken bouillon and egg. Mix well until heavy dough is formed.

Onto a floured surface, knead the dough for 3 minutes. Roll out into 1/8 inch thick and cut into mini squares. Place into greased baking sheet.

Bake for 15 minutes or until golden brown.

B CARROT BITES

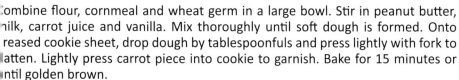

gredients:
cup whole wheat flour
cup cornmeal
cup wheat germ
cup peanut butter, creamy
cup milk, fat-free
cup carrot juice
tsp. vanilla
aby carrots, chopped for garnish

irections:
reheat oven to 350°F. Lightly spray baking
heet with nonstick cooking spray.

ombine flour, cornmeal and wheat germ in a large bowl. Stir in peanut butter,
ilk, carrot juice and vanilla. Mix thoroughly until soft dough is formed. Onto
reased cookie sheet, drop dough by tablespoonfuls and press lightly with fork to
atten. Lightly press carrot piece into cookie to garnish. Bake for 15 minutes or
ntil golden brown.

CARROT PUPCAKES

Ingredients:
1 cup whole wheat flour
1 cup cornmeal
1 cup carrots, finely shredded
1 tsp. cinnamon
1 tsp. vanilla
1 tbsp. honey
½ cup milk, fat-free
½ applesauce, unsweetened

Directions:
reheat oven to 350°F. Line mini
nuffin pan with mini muffin cups.
ightly spray cups with nonstick
ooking spray.

Frosting (Optional):
¼ cup cream cheese, nonfat & softened
1 tbsp. applesauce, unsweetened

ombine flour, cornmeal, carrots and cinnamon in a large bowl. Stir in vanilla,
oney, milk and applesauce. Mix well. Pour batter evenly into the greased muffin
ups. Bake for 15-20 minutes or until toothpick inserted in center comes out
lean. Allow to cool.

rosting (Optional):
ombine the frosting ingredients in a small bowl. Beat well until light and fluffy.
ipe or spoon frosting onto cooled muffins.

FRESH SQUASH PUPCAKES

Ingredients:
2 cups whole wheat flour
1 tsp. baking powder
1 tbsp. oil
1 cup carrot juice
1 tbsp. honey
1 medium zucchini, finely shredded
1 egg

Directions:
Preheat oven to 350°F. Lightly spray mini muffin pan with nonstick cooking spray.

Combine flour and baking powder in a large bowl. Stir in oil, carrot juice, honey, egg and zucchini. Mix thoroughly. Spoon batter onto greased muffin cups.

Bake for 20 minutes or until toothpick inserted in center comes out clean.

SALMON SPINACH CAKES

Ingredients:
1 cup whole wheat flour
1 cup oatmeal
1 cup spinach, cooked & drained
1 (4oz.) canned salmon
½ cup chicken broth
2 tbsp. oil
1 egg

Directions:
Preheat oven to 350°F. Lightly spray baking sheet with nonstick cooking spray.

In a large bowl, combine flour and oatmeal. Stir in spinach, salmon, broth, egg and oil. Mix well to form stiff dough.

On floured surface, knead dough for 3 minutes. Roll out into 1/2 inch thick and cut into squares. Place on greased baking sheet.

Bake for 15-20 minutes or until golden brown.

BBQ BONES

Ingredients:
2 cups whole wheat flour
¼ cup chicken, cooked & shredded
¼ cup tomato paste
2 tbsp. oil
⅛ cup molasses
½ cup chicken broth

Directions:
Preheat oven to 350°F. Lightly spray cookie sheet with nonstick cooking spray.

Combine all ingredients in a large bowl. Mix well until heavy dough is formed. On a floured surface, knead the dough for 3 minutes. Roll out to 1/4 inch thickness and cut with bone shaped cookie cutters. Place cookies onto greased cookie sheet.

Bake for 10-15 minutes or until done.

GREEN MONSTERS

Ingredients:
cup whole wheat flour
cup oatmeal
cup spinach, cooked & drained
tsp. chicken bouillon
cup Jack cheese, shredded
cup water

Directions:
Preheat oven to 350°F. Lightly spray cookie sheet with nonstick cooking spray.

Combine all ingredients in a large bowl. Mix well until stiff dough is formed. On a floured surface, knead dough for 2-3 minutes. Roll out to 1/2 inch thick and cut into strips using pizza cutter or sharp knife. Place strips onto greased cookie sheet. Bake for 15 minutes or until done.

YOGURT ZUCCHINI PUFFS

Ingredients:
2 cups whole wheat flour
1 tsp. baking powder
1 medium zucchini, shredded
1 tbsp. margarine
1 (6 oz.) plain yogurt
1 tbsp. vanilla
1 tbsp. oil
⅛ cup water

Directions:
Preheat oven to 350°F. Lightly spray muffin cups with nonstick cooking spray.

Combine all ingredients in a large bowl. Mix well until thoroughly blended. Spoon batter evenly onto greased muffin cups. Bake for 20-25 minutes.

HONEY LOAF

Dough 1:
Ingredients:
2 cups whole wheat flour
½ cup milk, fat-free
1 tbsp. honey
1 tbsp. molasses
1 tsp. vanilla

Dough 2 :
Ingredients:
1 cup all-purpose flour
¼ cup water

Filling:
Ingredients:
¼ cup carrots, shredded
¼ cup peanut butter, creamy
⅓ cup wheat germ
1 tbsp. oil

Directions:

Combine all of dough 1 ingredients and mix well until stiff dough is formed. Knead for 3 minutes and roll out dough into rectangle to about ¼ inch thick. Brush with water. Set aside.

Combine all of dough 2 ingredients and mix well until stiff dough is formed. Knead for 3 minutes and roll out into rectangle about 1/8 inch thick. Lay on top of dough 1. Brush with water. The lighter colored all-purpose flour provides a nice contrast.

In a bowl, mix all filling ingredients thoroughly. Spoon the mixture on top of dough 2. Roll tightly like a jelly roll and pinch seams and ends. Wrap in plastic wrap and chill in the freezer for an hour or until firm.

Heat oven to 375°F. Lightly spray cookie sheet with nonstick cooking spray. Remove rolls from plastic wrap. Cut loaf into 1/2 inch thick slices using serrated knife. Place slices onto greased cookie sheet. Bake for 20-25 minutes or until browned.

SWEET POTATO SLICES

Ingredients:
1 cup whole wheat flour
1 cup oat flour
1 medium sweet potato,
   cooked & mashed
1 tsp. vanilla
1 tbsp. honey
1 tbsp. oil
½ cup milk, fat-free

Directions:
Preheat oven to 350°F. Lightly spray cookie sheet with nonstick cooking spray.

Combine all the ingredients in a large bowl. Mix well until stiff dough is formed. Onto floured surface, knead dough for 3 minutes. Shape dough into a log about 1 inch diameter. Cut into manageable lengths and wrap in plastic wrap. Chill in the freezer for an hour or until firm.

Heat oven to 350°F. Lightly spray baking sheet with nonstick cooking spray. Remove rolls from plastic wrap.

Cut the log into 1/2 inch slices. Place on greased baking sheet.

Bake for 20-25 minutes or until dry.

VEGGIE CRUNCHIES

Ingredients:
1 cup whole wheat flour
1 cup oatmeal
¼ cup carrots, shredded
1 cup frozen broccoli, thawed & drained
1 cup vegetable/chicken broth
1 tbsp. oil
1 egg

Directions:
Preheat oven to 350°F. Lightly spray cookie sheet with nonstick cooking spray.

In a food processor, blend broccoli, carrots, oil, egg and broth. Transfer mixture to a large bowl. Stir in flour and oatmeal. Mix well. Onto greased cookie sheet, drop dough by tablespoonfuls and press with fork to slightly flatten.

Bake for 15 minutes or until edges are golden brown.

SQUASH PILLOWS

Ingredients:
2 cups whole wheat flour
1 medium zucchini, shredded
½ cup Cheddar cheese, shredded
1 tsp. chicken bouillon
½ cup water
2 tbsp. oil

Directions:
Preheat oven to 350°F. Lightly spray cookie sheet with nonstick cooking spray.

Combine all ingredients in a large bowl. Mix well until stiff dough is formed. On a floured surface, knead the dough for 2-3 minutes. Roll out to 1/2 inch thick and cut into cubes using pizza cutter or sharp knife. Place cubes onto greased cookie sheet.

Bake for 15 minutes or until done.

DINGO DELIGHTS

Ingredients:
1 cup whole wheat flour
1 cup oatmeal
1 cup Cheddar cheese, shredded
1 tsp. baking powder
1 tbsp. oil
1 egg, beaten
1 cup frozen spinach, thawed & drained
½ cup chicken broth

Directions:
Preheat oven to 350°F. Lightly spray cookie sheet with nonstick cooking spray.

In a large bowl, combine flour, oatmeal, baking powder, and cheese. Stir in oil, egg, spinach and chicken broth. Mix well until stiff dough is formed. On a floured surface, knead the dough for about 2-3 minutes. Roll out to 1/4 inch thick and cut into squares using pizza cutter or sharp knife. Place squares onto greased cookie sheet.

Bake for 15 minutes or until done.

EMPANADA YUMS

Ingredients:

Dough:
2 cups whole wheat flour
1 tsp. baking powder
2 tbsp. fresh parsley, minced
1 tbsp. oil
1 tbsp. honey
½ cup chicken broth

Filling:
1 cup frozen spinach, thawed & drained
½ cup chicken, cooked & shredded

Directions:

Preheat oven to 350°F. Lightly spray cookie sheet with nonstick cooking spray.

Combine all dough ingredients in a large bowl. Mix well until stiff dough is formed. On a floured surface, knead the dough for 2-3 minutes. Roll out to 1/4 inch thick and cut into rounds. Brush each round with water and set aside.

In a small bowl, mix the filling ingredients. Spoon 1 tablespoon of filling into center of each round. Fold rounds in half, pinch to seal and crimp edges with fork. Bake for 15-20 minutes or until done.

BAKED RICE FRITTERS

Ingredients:
1 cup whole wheat flour
1 cup rice flour
1 tsp. baking powder
½ cup brown rice, cooked
1 tsp. cinnamon
1 tsp. fresh parsley, minced
1 tbsp. molasses
1 cup chicken broth
1 egg

Directions:
Preheat oven to 350°F. Lightly spray cookie sheet with nonstick cooking spray.

Combine all ingredients in a large bowl. Mix well until soft dough is formed. Onto greased cookie sheet, drop dough by 2 tablespoonfuls. Bake for 20 minutes or until done.

APPLE OATMEAL CRUNCHIES

Ingredients:
1 cup whole wheat flour
2 cups oatmeal
1 tsp. baking powder
1 tsp. cinnamon
1 tsp. vanilla
1 tbsp. honey
1 ½ cup applesauce, unsweetened
1 medium apple, peeled & chopped

Directions:
Preheat oven to 350°F. Lightly spray cookie sheet with nonstick cooking spray.

In a large bowl, combine flour, oatmeal, baking powder and cinnamon. Add vanilla, honey and applesauce. Mix well. Stir in chopped apples until just blended. Onto greased cookie sheet, drop dough by tablespoonfuls and press with fork to slightly flatten.

Bake for 15 minutes or until edges are golden brown.

BERRY NICE COOKIES

Ingredients:
2 cups whole wheat flour
1 cup oatmeal
2 tsp. baking powder
1 tsp. cinnamon
1 cup canned pumpkin
1 tbsp. oil
1 egg
1 ¼ cups water
½ cup dried berries, cranberries & blueberries

Directions:
Preheat oven to 350°F. Lightly spray cookie sheet with nonstick cooking spray.

In a large bowl, combine flour, oatmeal, baking powder and cinnamon. Add pumpkin, oil, egg and water. Mix well. Stir in dried berries until just blended. Onto greased cookie sheet, drop dough by spoonfuls and press with fork to slightly flatten.

Bake for 10-15 minutes or until edges are golden brown.

CAROB PINWHEELS

Ingredients:

Dough 1:
1 cup whole wheat flour
1 cup cornmeal
1 tsp. baking powder
⅓ cup peanut butter
1 ¼ cups water
1 tsp. vanilla
1 egg

Dough 2:
1 cup whole wheat flour
1 cup oatmeal
¼ cup carob powder, unsweetened
1 tsp. cinnamon
2 tbsp. molasses
½ cup applesauce, unsweetened
1 tbsp. oil

Directions:
Combine all of dough 1 ingredients and mix well until stiff dough is formed. Knead for 3 minutes and roll out dough into rectangle to about 1/8 inch thick. Brush with water. Set aside.

Combine all of dough 2 ingredients and mix well until stiff dough is formed. Knead for 3 minutes and roll out into rectangle about 1/8 inch thick. Lay on top of dough 1. Brush with water. Roll tightly like a jelly roll and pinch seams and ends. Wrap in plastic wrap and chill in the freezer for an hour or until firm.

Heat oven to 375°F. Lightly spray cookie sheet with nonstick cooking spray. Remove rolls from plastic wrap. Slice roll of dough into 1 inch thick slices using serrated knife. Place slices into greased cookie sheet. Bake for 20-25 minutes or until brown.

BANANA NUT PUPCAKES

Ingredients:
1 cup whole wheat flour
1 cup rolled oats
1 tsp. baking powder
1 tsp. cinnamon
1 tbsp. oil
1 tsp. vanilla
1 banana, mashed
1 cup applesauce, unsweetened
⅛ cup pecans, chopped

Directions:
Preheat oven to 350°F. Lightly spray cupcake pan with nonstick cooking spray.

Combine all ingredients in a large bowl. Mix well until thoroughly blended. Pour batter into greased cupcake pan.

Bake for 20-25 minutes or until toothpick inserted in center comes out clean.

SQUASH BERRY MUFFINS

Ingredients:
1 cup whole wheat flour
1 cup cornmeal
1 tsp. baking powder
1 medium zucchini, shredded
2 tbsp. honey
1 egg, beaten
1 cup carrot juice
½ cup dried blueberries

Directions:
Preheat oven to 350°F. Lightly spray mini muffin pan with nonstick cooking spray.

In a large bowl, combine flour, cornmeal and baking powder. Stir in zucchini, honey, egg, carrot juice and blueberries. Mix well. Pour batter evenly into the greased muffin cups.

Bake for 15-20 minutes or until toothpick inserted in center comes out clean.

BERRY YOGURT COOKIES

Ingredients:
2 ¼ cups whole wheat flour
1 tsp. baking powder
1 (6 oz.) plain yogurt
2 tbsp. oil
¼ cup dried blueberries
¼ cup dried cranberries

Directions:
Preheat oven to 350°F. Lightly spray cookie sheet with nonstick cooking spray.

Combine all ingredients in a large bowl. Mix well until dough is formed. On a floured surface, knead the dough for 3 minutes. Roll out to 1/2 inch thick and cut into rounds. Place cookies onto greased cookie sheet.

Bake for 25 minutes or until firm.

BANANA BONES

Ingredients:
2 cups whole wheat flour
1 tsp. cinnamon
1 tsp. vanilla
1 banana, mashed
¼ cup peanut butter, creamy
1 tbsp. oil
1 cup milk, nonfat

Directions:
Preheat oven to 350°F. Lightly spray cookie sheet with nonstick cooking spray.

Combine all ingredients in a large bowl. Mix well until dough is formed. On a floured surface, knead the dough for 3 minutes. Roll out to 1/4 inch thickness and cut with bone shaped cookie cutters. Place cookies onto greased cookie sheet.

Bake for 10-15 minutes or until done.

CAROB MACAROONS

Ingredients:
½ cup whole wheat flour
½ cup wheat germ
¼ cup carob powder, unsweetened
¼ cup flaked coconut, unsweetened
1 egg
1 tbsp. molasses
¼ cup water

Directions:
Preheat oven 350°F. Lightly spray cookie sheet with nonstick cooking spray.

Combine all ingredients in a large bowl. Mix well. Onto greased cookie sheet, drop a tablespoonful of dough.

Bake for 15 minutes or until firm.

CHEWY GRANOLA COOKIES

Ingredients:
2 cups Granola, plain
1 cup whole wheat flour
1 tsp. baking powder
¼ cup dried berries, cranberry or blueberry
1 egg
1 tbsp. oil
1 cup carrot juice
½ cup milk, fat-free

Directions:
Preheat oven 350°F. Lightly spray cookie sheet with nonstick cooking spray.

Combine all ingredients in a large bowl. Mix well. Onto greased cookie sheet, drop tablespoonfuls of dough and press slightly with finger to flatten. Bake for 15 minutes or until firm.

PUMPKIN SPICE PUPCAKES

Ingredients:
1 cup whole wheat flour
1 cup rolled oats
1 cup canned pumpkin
2 tsp. baking powder
1 tsp. pumpkin-spice
1 tbsp. molasses
1 egg
¾ cup orange juice
¼ cup cranberry, dried

Directions:
Preheat oven 350°F. Line muffin pan with paper muffin cups. Spray paper cups with nonstick cooking spray.

Combine all ingredients in a large bowl. Mix well. Spoon batter into greased muffin cups. You may use mini muffin pans or regular sized muffin pans depending upon the size of your dog.

Bake for 15 minutes or until toothpick inserted in the center comes out clean.

BONEY MARONEYS

Ingredients:
2 cups whole wheat flour
1 cup oatmeal
1 cup canned pumpkin
1 tsp. cinnamon
1 tsp. vanilla
1 egg
½ cup milk, fat-free

Directions:
Preheat oven to 350°F. Lightly spray cookie sheet with nonstick cooking spray.

Combine all ingredients in a large bowl. Mix well until stiff dough is formed. On a floured surface, knead the dough for 3 minutes. Roll out to 1/4 inch thickness and cut with bone shaped cookie cutters. Place cookies onto greased cookie sheet. Bake for 10-15 minutes or until done.

CAROB ZUCCHINI CHIPS

Ingredients:
1 cup whole wheat flour
1 cup oat flour
1 tsp. baking powder
¼ cup carob powder, unsweetened
1 medium zucchini, shredded
1 tsp. vanilla
½ cup applesauce, unsweetened
1 egg, beaten

Directions:
Preheat oven to 350°F. Lightly spray cookie sheet with nonstick cooking spray.

In a large bowl, combine flours, baking powder and carob powder. Stir in zucchini, vanilla, applesauce and egg. Mix well until stiff dough is formed. On a floured surface, knead dough for 3 minutes. Roll out to 1/4 inch thickness and cut into tiny rounds. Place rounds onto greased cookie sheet. Poke cookies with a fork to texture. Bake for 10-15 minutes or until done.

PEANUT BUTTER BRAIDS

Ingredients:

2 cups whole wheat flour
⅓ cup peanut butter, creamy
½ cup milk, fat-free
¾ cup water
1 tsp. vanilla

1 tbsp. honey
1 egg
2 tbsp. oil
1 egg white, for egg wash

Directions:

Preheat oven to 350°F. Lightly spray baking sheet with nonstick cooking spray.

Combine all ingredients except egg white in a large bowl. Mix thoroughly until stiff dough is formed. On a floured surface, knead dough for 3 minutes. Roll out to 1/4 inch thick and cut into long strips using pizza cutter or sharp knife. Using three strips at a time lift outside strips and bring to center, alternating right and left side to create a braid. When finished press the end of the three strips together to keep it from unbraiding. Brush with egg wash. Place braids on a greased baking sheet.

Bake for 20 minutes or until done.

PUMPKIN BANANA PUPMUFFINS

Ingredients:
1 ½ cups whole wheat flour
1 cup oatmeal
1 tsp. baking powder
1 tsp. pumpkin-spice
1 banana, mashed
1 cup canned pumpkin
1 cup apple juice

Directions:
Preheat oven to 350°F. Lightly spray mini muffin pan with nonstick cooking spray.

Combine all ingredients in a large bowl. Mix well. Pour batter evenly into the greased muffin pan.

Bake for 15-20 minutes or until toothpick inserted in center comes out clean.

BROWN DOGS

Ingredients:

Dough:
2 cups whole wheat flour
1 cup oatmeal
1 tsp. baking powder
¼ cup carob powder, unsweetened
1 tbsp. molasses
1 tbsp. honey

2 tbsp. oil
½ cup milk, nonfat
1 cup water
1 egg

Filling:
½ cup nonfat cream cheese, softened
2 tbsp. applesauce

Directions:

Preheat oven to 350°F. Lightly spray baking sheet with nonstick cooking spray.

Combine all dough ingredients in a large bowl. Mix thoroughly until soft dough is formed. Onto greased baking sheet, drop dough by 2 table-spoonfuls and press with fork to slightly flatten. Bake for 15 minutes or until done. Allow to cool.

In a small bowl, beat cream cheese and applesauce until light and fluffy. Spread filling between two cooled cookies.

GOLDEN COOKIES

Ingredients:
2 cups whole wheat flour
1 cup oatmeal
1 tsp. pumpkin-pie spice
1 tsp. baking powder
1 ¼ cup carrot juice
1 tbsp. honey
¼ cup nonfat cream cheese, softened
2 tbsp. oil
1 egg, lightly beaten

Directions:
Preheat oven to 350°F. Lightly spray baking sheet with nonstick cooking spray.

In a large bowl, combine flour, oatmeal, pumpkin-pie spice, and baking powder. Stir in carrot juice, honey, cream cheese, oil and egg. Mix well. Onto greased baking sheet, drop dough by a tablespoonful. Tap cookie sheet from underneath to flatten cookies. Bake for 15 minutes or until edges are golden brown.

TWISTED TREATS

Ingredients:

Peanut Butter Dough:
2 cups whole wheat flour
⅓ cup peanut butter, creamy
1 ¼ cup water
1tsp. cinnamon
1 tbsp. honey
1 egg
1 tbsp. oil

Carob Dough:
2 cups whole wheat flour
¼ cup carob powder, unsweetened
½ cup water
1 tbsp. molasses
1 tbsp. oil
1 egg

Directions:

Preheat oven to 350°F. Lightly spray baking sheet with nonstick cooking spray.

Combine all peanut butter dough ingredients in a large bowl. Mix thoroughly until stiff dough is formed. On a floured surface, knead dough for 3 minutes. Roll out to 1/4 inch thick and brush with water. Set aside.

In the same bowl, combine all the carob dough ingredients. Mix well until stiff dough is formed. On a floured surface, knead dough for 3 minutes. Roll out to 1/4 inch thick and lay on top of the peanut butter dough. Press dough together using rolling pin. Roll out to a final thickness of 1/4 inch. Cut into 3/4 inch wide strips. Twist strips and place onto greased cookie sheet. Bake for 20 minutes or until done.

HONEY-GINGER STICKS

Ingredients:
1 cup whole wheat flour
1 cup cornmeal
1 tsp. ground ginger
2 tbsp. molasses
2 tbsp. honey
1 egg
½ cup water
2 tbsp. oil

Directions:
Preheat oven to 350°F. Lightly spray baking sheet with nonstick cooking spray.

Combine all ingredients in a large bowl. Mix thoroughly until stiff dough is formed. On a floured surface, knead dough for 3 minutes. Roll out to 1/2 inch thick and cut into 3 inches long strips using pizza cutter or sharp knife.

Bake for 15 minutes or until lightly browned.

DOGGY DONUTS

Ingredients:

2 cups whole wheat flour
1 cup oat flour
2 tsp. baking powder
1 tsp. cinnamon
1 tsp. vanilla

2 tbsp. oil
1 tbsp. honey
1 tbsp. molasses
1 egg
¾ cup applesauce, unsweetened

Directions:

Preheat oven to 350°F. Lightly spray cookie sheet with nonstick cooking spray.

Combine all ingredients in a large bowl. Mix well until stiff dough is formed. On a floured surface, knead the dough for 3 minutes. Roll out to 1/2 inch thick and cut with doughnut cutter or use 2 (large and small) round cutters. Place onto greased cookie sheet.

Bake for 20 minutes or until firm.

CAROB CHIP COOKIES

Ingredients:
2 cups whole wheat flour
½ cup carob chips, unsweetened
1 tsp. baking powder
1 tsp. cinnamon
1 tbsp. molasses
1 egg
¾ cup water

Directions:
Preheat oven to 350°F. Lightly spray baking sheet with nonstick cooking spray.

In a large bowl, combine all ingredients and mix well. Onto greased cookie sheet, drop dough by a tablespoonful.

Bake for 15 minutes or until edges are golden brown.

GINGER CRÈME COOKIES

Ingredients:
1 cup whole wheat flour
1 cup cornmeal
2 tsp. ground ginger
2 tbsp. molasses
½ cup chicken broth
2 tbsp. oil

Filling:
½ cup nonfat cream cheese, softened
2 tbsp. applesauce, unsweetened

Directions:
Preheat oven to 350°F. Lightly spray baking sheet with nonstick cooking spray.

Combine all dough ingredients in a large bowl. Mix thoroughly until stiff dough is formed. On a floured surface, knead dough for 3 minutes. Roll out to 1/4 inch thick and cut into rounds. Slightly press fork on dough to add texture. Place rounds onto a greased baking sheet.

Bake for 15 minutes or until done. Allow to cool.

In a small bowl, beat cream cheese and applesauce until light and fluffy. Spread filling between two cooled cookies.

OUND CAKES

gredients:
cup whole wheat flour
cup oatmeal
tsp. baking powder
tsp. pumpkin-pie spice
cup canned pumpkin
 cup orange juice
egg, beaten
tbsp. oil
cup pecan, chopped for garnish

irections:
reheat oven to 350°F. Line mini muffin
an with paper cups. Lightly spray paper
ups with nonstick cooking spray.

ombine flour, oatmeal, baking powder and pumpkin-pie spice in a large bowl.
tir in pumpkin, juice, egg and oil. Mix well. Pour batter into the greased muffin
ups. Slightly press pecan on top using spoon to garnish. Bake for 15-20 minutes
r until toothpick inserted in center comes out clean.

HAPPY TAILS MUFFINS

Ingredients:
1 cup whole wheat flour
1 cup cornmeal
1 tsp. baking powder
½ cup Cheddar cheese, shredded
1 tsp. vanilla
½ cup nonfat cream cheese, softened
½ cup applesauce, unsweetened
1 egg

Directions:
Preheat oven to 350°F. Line mini muffin
pan with paper cups. Lightly spray paper
cups with nonstick cooking spray.

Combine flour, cornmeal, baking powder
nd 1/4 cup Cheddar cheese in a large bowl. Stir in vanilla, cream cheese, apple-
auce and egg. Mix well. Pour batter evenly into the greased muffin cups. Spoon
he remaining ¼ cup of Cheddar cheese on top of the muffins and press lightly
with your fingers. Bake for 15-20 minutes or until done.

GINGER LOGS

Ingredients:
2 cups whole wheat flour
2 tsp. ground ginger
2 tbsp. molasses
1 tsp. chicken bouillon
1 egg
½ cup milk, nonfat
2 tbsp. oil

Glaze (Optional):
½ cup yogurt chips

Directions:
Preheat oven to 350°F. Lightly spray baking sheet with nonstick cooking spray.

Combine all ingredients in a large bowl. Mix thoroughly until stiff dough is formed. On a floured surface, knead dough for 3 minutes. Roll out to 1/2 inch thick and cut into strips using pizza cutter or sharp knife. Place onto greased cookie sheet.

Bake for 15 minutes or until lightly browned. Allow to cool. In a microwaveable bowl, microwave yogurt chips for 1 minute. Stir until smooth and creamy. Dip one end of logs into melted yogurt. Let it dry on waxed paper.

PEANUT BUTTER BARS

Ingredients:
1 cup whole wheat flour
1 cup oatmeal
1 tsp. cinnamon
½ cup peanut butter, creamy
1 tsp. vanilla
2 tbsp. honey
½ cup apple juice
¾ cup water

Directions:
Preheat oven to 350°F. Lightly spray baking sheet with nonstick cooking spray.

Combine all ingredients in a large bowl. Mix thoroughly until stiff dough is formed. On a floured surface, knead dough for 3 minutes. Roll out to 1/2 inch thick and cut into rectangles using pizza cutter or sharp knife. Place onto greased cookie sheet.

Bake for 20 minutes or until lightly browned.

JAKE'S FAVORITE COOKIES

Ingredients:
Dough:
2 cups whole wheat flour
1 tsp. baking powder
1 tsp. chicken bouillon
⅓ cup peanut butter, creamy
2 tbsp. oil
1 egg

½ cup milk, nonfat
¾ cup water

Filling:
⅓ cup peanut butter, creamy
¼ cup wheat germ
1 tbsp. oil

Directions:
Preheat oven to 350°F. Lightly spray baking sheet with nonstick cooking spray.

Combine all dough ingredients in a large bowl. Mix thoroughly until stiff dough is formed. On a floured surface, knead dough for 3 minutes. Roll out to 1/4 inch thick and cut into rounds. Place rounds onto a greased baking sheet.

Bake for 15 minutes or until done. Allow cookies to cool.

In a small bowl, mix peanut butter, oil and wheat germ thoroughly. Spread filling between two cooled cookies.

BERRY NANA CAKES

Ingredients:
1 cup whole wheat flour
1 cup oat flour
1 tsp. baking powder
1 tsp. cinnamon
1 tsp. vanilla
2 tbsp. honey
1 banana, mashed
1 egg, beaten
1 cup applesauce, unsweetened
½ cup dried blueberries

Directions:
Preheat oven to 350°F. Lightly spray mini muffin cups with nonstick cooking spray.

Combine all ingredients in a large bowl. Mix well. Pour batter evenly into the greased muffin cups.

Bake for 15-20 minutes or until toothpick inserted in center comes out clean.

OATMEAL BARKS

Ingredients:
2 cups whole wheat flour
1 cup oatmeal
1 tsp. baking powder
2 tbsp. oil
1 egg
¾ cup apple juice

Directions:
Preheat oven to 350°F. Lightly spray cookie sheet with nonstick cooking spray.

Combine flour, baking powder, oil, egg and juice in a large bowl. Mix well until stiff dough is formed. Knead dough for about a minute on a lightly floured surface. Sprinkle the oatmeal on the work surface. Roll dough to coat with oatmeal. Roll out to 1/2 inch thick and cut into squares using pizza cutter or sharp knife. Place squares onto greased cookie sheet.

Bake for 20 minutes or until done.

HOME SWEET HOME

Ingredients:
1 ½ cup whole wheat flour
1 cup oat flour
1 tsp. chicken bouillon
½ cup applesauce, unsweetened
1 medium zucchini, shredded
1 egg, lightly beaten

Directions:
Preheat oven to 350°F.

In a large bowl, combine all dry ingredients. Add applesauce, zucchini and egg. Mix well until dough is formed.

On a floured surface, knead dough for about 3 minutes. Add more flour if necessary to make stiff dough. Roll out to 1/2 inch thick and cut into dog houses using supplied cookie cutter.

Place onto a greased baking sheet. Bake for 15 minutes or until golden brown.

HOUND DOG HARVEST

Ingredients:
1 cup whole wheat flour
1 cup cornmeal
½ cup wheat germ
1 tsp. baking powder
2 tbsp. molasses
¼ cup water
1 cup orange juice
1tsp. vanilla
½ cup dried cranberries
¼ cup flaxseed for garnish (optional)

Directions:
Preheat oven to 350°F. Lightly spray muff
pan with nonstick cooking spray.

Combine flour, cornmeal, wheat germ and baking powder in a large bowl. Stir
molasses, water, orange juice and vanilla. Mix well and fold in cranberries. Po
batter evenly into the greased muffin cups. Spoon flaxseed on top and pre
slightly with your fingers.

Bake for 15-20 minutes or until toothpick inserted in center comes out clean.

MUTTS MACAROONS

Ingredients:
1 cup whole wheat flour
1 banana, mashed
½ cup coconut flakes, unsweetened
¼ cup water

Directions:
Preheat oven to 350°F. Lightly spray
cookie sheet with nonstick cooking
spray.

Combine all ingredients in a large
bowl and mix well. Onto greased cookie
sheet, drop dough by a tablespoonful and
press with your fingers to slightly flatten.

Bake for 15 minutes or until edges are golden brown.

PRETZEL TREATS

Ingredients:
2 cups whole wheat flour
1 cup cornmeal
1 cup wheat germ
¾ cup peanut butter, creamy
2 tbsp. honey
2 tbsp. oil
2 ½ cups water

Directions:
Preheat oven to 350°F. Lightly spray cookie sheet with nonstick cooking spray.

In a large bowl, combine flour, cornmeal, and wheat germ. Stir in peanut butter, honey, oil and water. Mix well until stiff dough is formed. On a floured surface, knead the dough for 3 minutes. Tear off some dough and roll a long rope about 1/2 inch diameter. Pick up both ends; make a loop at the center. Add a twist and bring the ends over to form a traditional pretzel shape. Place pretzels onto greased cookie sheet.

Bake for 20 minutes or until done.

YAPPIN' YAM ROLLS

Ingredients:

Dough:
2 ½ cups whole wheat flour
1 medium sweet potato,
    cooked and mashed
1 tsp. baking powder
1 tsp. cinnamon

1 egg
1 tbsp. oil
½ cup milk, nonfat

Filling:
½ cup nonfat cream cheese, softened
¼ cup oatmeal

Directions:
Combine all of dough ingredients and mix well until stiff dough is formed. Knea
for 3 minutes and roll out dough into rectangle to about 1/4 inch thick. Set aside

Combine all the filling ingredients and mix well. Spread filling mixture evenly ont
the dough. Roll tightly like a jelly roll. Pinch seams and ends to seal. Wrap in plast
wrap and chill in the freezer for an hour or until firm.

Heat oven to 350°F. Lightly spray cookie sheet with nonstick cooking spra
Remove rolls from plastic wrap. Cut roll of dough into 1/2 inch thick slices usir
serrated knife. Place slices onto greased cookie sheet.

Bake for 20-25 minutes or until browned.

HOUNDSTOOTH SCONES

Ingredients:

cup whole
wheat flour
cup cornmeal
tsp. baking powder
tsp. baking soda
cup Cheddar
cheese, shredded

1 tsp. chicken
bouillon
2 tbsp. molasses
½ cup water
1 egg

Glaze (Optional):
½ cup carob chips or
½ cup yogurt chips

Directions:

Preheat oven to 350°F. Lightly spray baking sheet with nonstick cooking spray.

Combine flour, cornmeal, baking powder, baking soda, cheese and chicken bouillon in a large bowl. Stir in molasses, egg and water until dough forms. Onto a floured surface, knead dough for 3 minutes. Roll out into ½ inch thick and cut into triangles using a pizza cutter or sharp knife. Bake for 20 minutes or until lightly browned. Allow to cool.

In a microwave or double-boiler, melt carob chips or yogurt chips. Stir until carob or yogurt chips are melted and smooth. Dip cooled scones halfway into the melted chips. Place on waxed paper until set.

ICED SCONES

Ingredients:

1 cup whole
 wheat flour
1 cup wheat germ
⅓ cup peanut
 butter, creamy
2 tbsp. honey

2 tbsp. oil
¼ cup milk, nonfat
1 cup water
1 egg

Glaze (Optional):
½ cup yogurt chips

Directions:
Preheat oven to 350°F. Lightly spray baking sheet with nonstick cooking spray.

Combine all ingredients in a large bowl. Mix well until stiff dough is formed. Onto floured surface, knead dough for 3 minutes. Roll out to ½ inch thick and cut into triangles using a pizza cutter or sharp knife. Place onto greased baking sheet. Bake for 20 minutes or until lightly browned. Allow to cool.

In a microwave or double-boiler, melt yogurt chips. Stir until smooth and creamy. You may add a drop or two of beet juice to yogurt chips to make a nice pink color. Drizzle cooled scones with the melted chips and let them dry on waxed paper.

POODLE TAILS

Ingredients:
3 cups whole wheat flour
½ cup carob powder, unsweetened
1 tsp. ground ginger
3 tbsp. honey

1 tsp. cinnamon
¼ cup coconut milk, light
¾ cup water

Glaze (Optional):
½ cup yogurt chips

Directions:
Preheat oven to 350°F. Lightly spray baking sheet with nonstick cooking spray.

Combine all ingredients in a large bowl. Mix well until stiff dough is formed. Divide dough in half. Shape each half into 9x5 inch rectangle about 1/2 inch thick and place on a cookie sheet.

Bake for 25 minutes or until firm. Cool on cookie sheet for about 10 minutes. Slice rectangle crosswise about 3 inches long. Place slices back to the cookie sheet turning slices cut side up. Bake for another 15 minutes, turning once until firm. Cool completely.

Melt yogurt chips in a microwave or double-boiler. Stir until smooth. Add a drop or two of beet juice to make a nice pink color. Dip one end of each cooled biscotti about halfway into melted yogurt chips and let dry on waxed paper.

CORNY DOG COOKIES

Ingredients:
2 cups flour
1 cup wheat germ
½ cup corn, cooked
1 tsp. chicken bouillon
1 tbsp. honey
1 (6 oz.) baby food, vegetable flavor*
¾ cups water

Directions:
Preheat oven to 300°F. Lightly spray baking sheet with nonstick cooking spray.

Combine all ingredients in a large bowl. Mix well until stiff dough is formed. Onto a floured surface, knead dough for 3 minutes. Roll out into 1/4 inch thick and cut into fun shapes. Place onto greased baking sheet. Bake for 20-25 minutes or until dried.

*Other flavors can be substituted if desired.

FRIED BALONEY!

Ingredients:
Flour Tortillas
½ cup beet juice

Directions:
Ha Ha Ha! They're not baloney at all! They're just for fun. Cut tortillas into rounds. Dip into beet juice and slightly brown in a nonstick pan. It's quick and easy and a great little treat.

FROZEN TREATS

On hot summer days these desserts can be a refreshing reward. Watered dow
fruits are great. Try blending leftover chicken or a spoonful of pasta with a cup o
water. Dogs are happy and entertained with mostly water and just a hint of
yummy taste. Remember that they can smell 100 times better than humans.

CARROT FROZEN TREAT

Ingredients:
¼ cup cottage cheese, nonfat
¼ cup carrots, shredded
½ cup baby food, strained vegetable:
2 tbsp. honey
1 ½ cups water

Directions:
Blend cottage cheese, carrots, bab
food and honey in a food processo
Transfer pureed mixture into a larg
bowl and stir in water. Ladle mixtur
into serving cups and freeze.

BERRY FROZEN TREAT

Ingredients:
6 oz. plain yogurt
¼ cup blueberries, fresh
1 ½ cups carrot juice
1 tbsp. honey

Directions:
In a food processor, blend all
ingredients. Place pureed mixture
into serving cups and freeze.

PEANUT BUTTER FROZEN TREAT

Ingredients:
½ cup peanut butter, creamy
½ cup wheat germ
2 cups apple juice
1 tsp. chicken bouillon

Directions:
Combine all ingredients until well-blended. Spoon the mixture into serving cups and freeze.

BANANA SPLIT FROZEN TREAT

Ingredients:
 banana, mashed
 cup carob powder, unsweetened
 cups water

Directions:
Combine all ingredients and mix well. Transfer mixture into serving cups and freeze.

TUNA FROZEN TREAT

Ingredients:
½ cup canned tuna, in water
¼ cup carrots, shredded
2 cups chicken broth

Directions:
Blend all ingredients in a blender or food processor. Transfer pureed mixture into serving cups and freeze.

CEREAL TREATS

Using out of the box cereals can make your treats taste and look more interesting. There are many wholesome, whole grain cereals available on your supermarket shelves. Mix them with a binder such as eggs, bananas, or well cooked rice or oatmeal. Get creative and have fun. We recommend that you do not use sugared cereals.

CHEESY O's

Ingredients:
3 cups cereals of your choice
¼ cup Cheddar cheese, shredded
1 egg, beaten

Directions:
Preheat oven to 275°F. Spray muffin pan with nonstick cooking spray.

In a large bowl, combine cheese and egg. Mix well. Gently fold in cereals and mix carefully and quickly. Without delay, spoon mixture into greased muffin pan. Bake for 8-10 minutes.

NUTTY COOKIES

Ingredients:

Dough:	Garnish:
2 cups whole wheat flour	⅛ cup honey
1 tsp. baking powder	½ cup cereal of your choice
1 tsp. cinnamon	
½ cup water	
2 tbsp. oil	

Directions:
Preheat oven to 350°F. Lightly spray baking sheet with nonstick cooking spray.

In a large bowl, combine all dough ingredients. Mix well until heavy dough is formed. On a floured surface, knead dough for 3 minutes. Roll out to 1/4 inch thick and cut into rounds. Place rounds into greased baking sheet. Garnish the top of each round with honey and cereal. Bake for 15 minutes or until done.

CAROB PILLOWS

Ingredients:
½ cup carob chips
½ cup peanut butter, creamy
1 ½ cup cereal of your choice

Directions:
Combine carob chips and peanut butter in a microwaveable bowl. microwave for 1 minute. Stir until smooth and creamy. Stir in cereal until well-coated. Drop 2 tablespoonfuls into greased paper cups. Chill until firm.

NUTTY SPINNERS

Ingredients:

Dough:
cup whole wheat flour
cup cornmeal
cup milk, nonfat
egg

Filling:
1 cup cereal of your choice
2 tbsp. molasses
½ cup applesauce, unsweetened

Directions:
Combine all dough ingredients and mix well. Knead dough for 3 minutes and roll out to rectangle 1/8 inch thick. Brush with water. Set aside.

In a bowl, combine all the filling ingredients and mix well. Spread filling on top of the dough and roll tightly like a jelly roll. Pinch seams and ends. Wrap in plastic wrap and chill in the freezer for an hour or until firm.

Heat oven to 375°F. Lightly spray baking sheet with nonstick cooking spray. Remove from plastic wrap. Slice roll of dough into 1 inch thick using serrated knife. Place slices into baking sheet. Bake for 20-25 minutes or until browned.

CORN PUFFS

Ingredients:
4 cups cereal of your choice
1 egg
⅛ cup milk

Directions:
Preheat oven to 275°F. Spray muffin pan with nonstick cooking spray.

In a large bowl, blend egg and milk. Stir in cereal quickly until well-coated. Spoon mixture into greased muffin pan. The objective is to coat the cereal and spoon into the muffin pan before the cereal loses its shape. Bake for 10 minutes or until golden brown.

KIBBLE TREATS

Yes, treats can actually be made from your dog's own kibble food. The kibble used as a substitute for dough. This concept is especially beneficial for dogs th are on strict diets. By using a binder such as eggs, bananas, well cooked rice oatmeal, kibble can be transformed into cookies, cupcakes and brownies.

KIBBLE BROWNIES

Ingredients:
5 cups kibble
½ cup applesauce, unsweetened
1 cup apple juice
2 cups oatmeal
1 egg
1 tsp. vanilla

Directions:
Preheat oven to 250°F. Lightly spr. brownie pan* with nonstick cooki spray.

Combine all ingredients in a large bowl. Mix thoroughly until kibble is well-coate Transfer mixture onto greased brownie pan. Bake for 2 hours. Allow to cool for z hour. Remove the kibble cake from the pan. Cut into bite sized squares.

*The kibble recipes can be removed easily from silicon bake pans.

QUICK KIBBLE CHUNKS

Ingredients:
5 cups kibble
2 eggs
1 cup water

Directions:
Preheat oven to 250°F. Lightly spray brownie pan with nonstick cooking spray.

Combine all ingredients in a large bowl. Mix thoroughly. Transfer mixture into greased brownie pan. Bake for 2 hours. Remove from oven and allow to cool for an hour. Break into bite size treats.

CRISPY KIBBLE BITES

Ingredients:
5 cups kibble
2 eggs
1 cup applesauce, unsweetened
1 cup water

Directions:
Preheat oven to 225°F. Lightly spray brownie pan with nonstick cooking spray. Combine all ingredients in a large bowl. Mix thoroughly for a full 5 minutes. Transfer mixture into greased brownie pan.

Bake for 2 hours at 225°F and additional hour at 175°F. Remove from oven and allow to cool. Break into bite size treats.

SOUPER KIBBLE CUPCAKES

Ingredients:
5 cups kibble
1 (18.5 oz.) canned chicken noodle soup
2 eggs

Directions:
Preheat oven to 250°F. Generously spray cupcake pan with nonstick cooking spray. In a large bowl, combine all ingredients. Mix well until kibble is well-coated. Spoon kibble mixture into a greased or silicone cupcake pan. Bake for 2 hours.

BANANA KIBBLE CUPCAKES

Ingredients:
5 cups kibble
1 cup oatmeal
2 ripe bananas, mashed
1 cup water

Directions:
Preheat oven to 250°F. Generously spray cupcake pan with nonstick cooking spray.

In a large bowl, blend bananas and water. Stir in oatmeal and kibble and mix well. Pour kibble mixture into greased cupcake pan. Use a spoon to pack tightly into cupcake pan. Bake for 2 hours.

VEGAN TREATS

If you are a Vegan, there are many treats that can be made without meats. To¹
available in small bricks in the supermarket. It can be prepared in so many w
and even comes pre-seasoned if you wish. Tofu can be cut into tiny bits & use
treats as is or you can use it in the following recipes. Combine Tofu v
vegetables and dough to make the healthiest treats of all. Have fun!

VEGAN BONES

Ingredients:
1 cup whole wheat flour
1 cup oatmeal
½ cup wheat germ
1 banana
½ cup blueberry, fresh
1 tbsp. olive oil
1 cup almond milk

Directions:
Preheat oven to 350°F. Lightly spr
cookie sheet with nonstick cooki
spray.

In a food processor, blend banana, blueberries, olive oil and almond milk. Transf
mixture to a large bowl. Stir in flour, wheat germ and oatmeal. Mix well un
heavy dough is formed. On a floured surface, knead dough for 3 minutes. Roll o
to ¼ inch thickness and cut with bone shaped cookie cutters. Place cookies on
greased cookie sheet. Bake for 15-20 minutes or until done.

TOFU TURNOVER

Ingredients:

Dough:
3 cups whole wheat flour
2 tbsp. olive oil
1 tbsp. maple syrup
¾ cup water

Filling:
Tofu, cut into
thin squares

Directions:
Preheat oven to 350°F. Lightly grease
baking sheet with nonstick cooking
spray.

Combine all dough ingredients in a
large bowl. Mix well until stiff dough is
formed. On a floured surface, knead
dough for 3 minutes. Roll out to 1/8 inch thick and cut into 1 1/2 inch square
Sandwich 1 inch square thin slices of tofu between moistened dough square
Seal edges using fork. Bake for 20-25 minutes or until done.

SIMPLY VEGAN

Ingredients:
Dough:
2 cups whole wheat flour
⅓ cup peanut butter
1 banana, mashed
1 cup water

Glaze (Optional):
½ cup carob chips, unsweetened

Directions:
Preheat oven to 350°F. Lightly spray baking sheet with nonstick cooking spray.

In a large bowl, combine all dough ingredients and mix well. Knead dough for 3 minutes and roll out into 1/4 inch thick. Cut into bones and place on baking sheet. Bake for 15 minutes. In a double-boiler, melt carob chips. Stir until smooth. Dip cooled cookies into melted carob chips. Place on waxed paper to dry.

TOFU FRIES

Ingredients: Blocks of Tofu

Directions: Preheat oven to 300°F. Spray baking sheet with nonstick cooking spray. Slice blocks of tofu into long strips. Place strips onto baking sheet and season if desired. Bake for 30 minutes, flip strips over and bake for another 30 minutes or until tofu is dry.

SPINACH TREATS

Ingredients:
2 cups whole wheat flour
½ cup tofu
½ cup spinach, cooked & drained
¼ cup tomato paste
2 tbsp. olive oil
1 cup water

Directions:
Preheat oven to 350°F. Grease baking sheet with nonstick cooking spray.

In a food processor, blend tofu, spinach, tomato paste, water and olive oil. Transfer pureed mixture into a large bowl. Stir in flour and mix well. Knead dough for 3 minutes. Roll out into ¼ inch thick. Cut into your favorite shaped cookies. Place cookies onto baking sheet. Bake for 15 minutes or until done.

We do not advocate feeding your dog large quantities of treats. They should never be a substitute for food.

Treats are best used as barter. "Thanks for peeing outside & here's your reward".

If your dog is on a restricted diet consult your veterinarian before serving our recipes. Take care to avoid foods or ingredients that are known to cause allergic reactions in your pet.

Keeping your pet safe....

Some foods that are considered good for people can be very dangerous for pets.

The list below highlights some of the most common foods that can be dangerous to dogs. This is not an exhaustive list and any decision to provide your pet with food not specifically intended for animals should be discussed with your veterinarian or pet nutritionist.

Alchohol
Apple seeds
Apricot pits
Avocados
Bones
Cherry pits
Chocolate
Coffee
Citrus oil extracts
Dairy products
Eggplant

Garlic
Grapes
Macadamia nuts
Marijuana
Moldy foods
Mushrooms
Mustard seeds
Nutmeg
Peach pits
Onions
Onion powder

Raisins
Raw eggs
Raw fish
Raw meat or poultry
Raw potatoes
Rhubarb
Tea
Tomato leaves
Walnuts
Xylitol (sweetner)
Yeast dough

Certain foods, while not considered toxic, can still be unhealthy and should be consumed in moderation. Avoid any foods that are high in fat or sodium. Sugar should never be a part of your dog's diet. Corn cobs and bones can cause GI obstruction. Cooked bones may splinter and break easily, risking GI damage. These foods can contribute to obesity, indigestion, electrolyte imbalance, dehydration and more. Dairy products may be difficult for dogs to digest.

Index

Meat, Fish & Cheese

Veggies